Filthy Garments

Filthy Garments

Prophetess Sonya James

Filthy Garments

Copyright © 2020 by Prophetess Sonya James. All rights reserved.

No part of this publication may be reproduced, stored in a retrieval system or transmitted in any way by any means, electronic, mechanical, photocopy, recording or otherwise without the prior permission of the author except as provided by USA copyright law.

This novel is a work of fiction. Names, descriptions, entities, and incidents included in the story are products of the author's imagination. Any resemblance to actual persons, events, and entities is entirely coincidental.

The opinions expressed by the author are not necessarily those of URLink Print and Media.

1603 Capitol Ave., Suite 310 Cheyenne, Wyoming USA 82001
1-888-980-6523 | admin@urlinkpublishing.com

URLink Print and Media is committed to excellence in the publishing industry.

Book design copyright © 2020 by URLink Print and Media. All rights reserved.

Published in the United States of America

ISBN 978-1-64753-250-5 (Paperback)
ISBN 978-1-64753-251-2 (Digital)

25.02.20

Filthy Garments

It is time to enter your destiny!
Aren't you tired of being in the place called there?
Enter and be instantly changed.

It is your new day!
It is your new season!

Prophetess Sonya James

Acknowledgments

First and foremost, I thank my lord and savior Jesus Christ. And I thank God for His dear son who died for us that we may live and for delivering my life and expressing Himself in and through me. I am humbled and in awe of Him.

I want to thank my mother for her prayers and her continued example of strength to me and her love and faith in God.

I thank my children (Alexandra and Ruben-Elijah) who allow me to be who God would have me to be, and I thank them for their selfless attitude concerning my purpose and ministry, lending me to the world and encouraging and supporting me.

To my apostle, spiritual father, covering, and mentor, [Apostle R.L. Jackson] who stands in the gap for me, my family as well as the world. I thank God for you, your teachings of God, and your unconditional, unfailing love for me and my family, as well as the body of Christ.

To First Lady Jackson, for her prayers.

And to the countless people of God who have blessed my life and ministry, thank you and may God bless you as much as you have blessed me.

And hope maketh not ashamed; because the love of God is shed abroad in our hearts by the Holy Ghost which is given unto us. (Rom. 5:5, KJV)

Contents

Foreword 11
Prophets Pen 13
Introduction 15

Chapter 1: Freedom of Faith 17
Chapter 2: Indictments 20
Chapter 3: Pressing On 25
Chapter 4: The Branch 33
Chapter 5: The True Vine 39
Chapter 6: Wild Grapes 42
Chapter 7: Well-Beloved 50
Chapter 8: New Again 53

Foreword

Rediscovering the plan of God for your life can be wonderful and at times very frightening. This requires courage. You must trust that as you walk through the valley of your deliverance, you will come out on the other side whole. It is time for you to be undressed from what the devil has pronounced over your life.

Prophetess Sonya James is a woman of God that does not take down and believes in assaulting the walls of the enemy to tear the devil's kingdom down. This Woman of God is a gift to the Body of Christ weekly with her radio program every Thursday @ 3:15pm on wokbradio 1680 am station. If you have not been able to hear Radio Program, please tune in to be blessed by streaming live [www.wokbradio.com] or download app. God has gifted this Woman of God to be an anointed scribe, prophetic psalmist, song writer as well as a Prophetic voice in this decade. You will be greatly inspired and encouraged and empowered: for her message as God's Prophet/Seer is to "Bring God to the People: and The People back to God." God's manifestation, presence and power is released upon His people for the restoration he has ordered up for their lives every time God brings her forth in assignment: so this [3rd] book is just another avenue God is using to bring deliverance to his people. Other books are on Amazon and BN: "Get out of the Grave and Cross the Bridge/The Soulish Realm "Get Up from There. So, we encourage those who are seeking an impartation from God to get in the zone of [quietness] and let's take the next step to your [Deliverance].

To God be the glory*

God can remove what the enemy has dressed you with. "The devil lied to you." Enter in and be blessed, changed and finally free!

There are many garments that we find ourselves wearing as the years and the trials and tribulations roll on by. Look inside yourself as you read these pages that God himself has blessed to be written just for you. Do not read with your eyes shut; leave them open. Open the eyes of your mind and heart, as well as your soul, for it is in this position of honesty that you will find true deliverance, real deliverance. Dare to enter in and you will choose to be *delivered mind, body soul and spirit.*

It is so pivotal in this season of your life to grab hold of what God is about to speak to you. Take seriously your time with God. Get that quiet place and let Him do spiritual surgery where no one else can reach. I applaud you because the work you are about to do is worth the results.

Love your friend,

Prophetess Sonya James

Introduction

Several months ago, the Lord began to reveal some things to me. I had to minister in a church in North Carolina. And I have learned, being apostolically and prophetically anointed, that you can be in a room with a lot of people and they can miss the entire movement of what God is saying, thereby missing their very deliverance. This was during the summer of 2011 when God dropped this word into my spirit.

What Is Your Word?

—Hebrews 4:12–13 [12] For the word of God is quick and powerful, and sharper than any two-edged sword, piercing even to the dividing asunder of soul and spirit, and of the joints and marrow, and is the discerner of the thoughts and intents of the heart.

[13] Neither is there any creature that is not manifest in his sight: but all things are naked and opened unto the eyes of him with whom we must do.

This scripture is so powerfully spoken because the word of God's manifestations happens so suddenly that once it can be applied to your situation there is an instant and impactive impartation from God. But the key to this is that] you first must be honest about the fact that you need help. I am, through the Holy Spirit, going to break this down to you. It is time for change of *garments*, change of *raiment*. Your inner man can be revived, renewed, and restored by the power of God's word.

For you, this is my affirmation and declaration that your miracle change has already began. We affirm God's word, and He confirms His word with signs and wonders following. Be blessed and inspired by this gift from God to you.

1
Freedom of Faith

When I first began this journey with the Lord, I was broken, damaged by the world, and there was no hope inside me for the future. But I have come to know that the devil who spoke those things to me is a liar. The scripture that I previously spoke of is one that covers the wall of every church and the mouth of every believer, yet people are still the same as they were, never coming into the fullness of the Lord Jesus Christ.

We should never read the Word as if it were a story.
2 Cor. 3:6 (KJV) reads, "Who also hath made us able ministers of the new testament; not of the letter but of the spirit; for the letter killeth, but the spirit giveth life."

The Bible is not just a bunch of letters to be rehearsed. The Word of God is life to us. "He that hath an ear to hear let him hear" what the spirit of the Lord God is saying. Hebrews 4:12 (AMP) tells us,

For the Word that God speaks is alive and full of power[making it active, operative, energizing, and effective]; it s sharper than any two-edged sword, penetrating to the dividing line of the breath of life (soul) and [the immortal] spirit, and of joints and marrow [of the deepest parts of our nature], exposing and sifting and analyzing and judging the very thoughts and purposes of the heart.

I chose to use this version to further bring out how powerful and precise the word of God is.

One of the first things you must realize and understand is that the Word of God tells us in Proverbs 4:7 (KJV), "Wisdom is the principle thing; therefore, get wisdom: and with all thy getting get an understanding." It is something that I see so often—how an individual does not want to be honest about their situation of where their life is, for whatever reason, and will lie to their own selves. So, when the Holy Ghost comes to save and deliver, you can either receive it or not. But "wisdom crieth out she utters her voice in the streets."

The word *quick* means to move rapidly, speedily, or reacting immediately and sharply or powerfully. It also speaks to us about being effective or potent, having the capability to exert power, to be clearly defined or distinct, which is basically to have a sharp difference in *perception*. Your perception of God, your relationship with God, and your life is very important. The scripture goes on to tell us that the Word of God is a "two-edged sword" (Heb. 4:12, KJV). To some that may mean that no matter what, on either end, you lose. No! That is a lie! Because the word of God is the sharp difference between life and death, truth and lie. His word is sharper than any sword or verdict made by the enemy or anyone else concerning your life. *God is always the final answer!*

When I began to study out this Word of God, the word *sword* is what God brought out to me for you. You see there will be many verdicts that the enemy will attempt to place against us, but once you can get

> ***"The right perception is the sharp difference that will penetrate your situation and your life."***

Maybe you are dealing with disease, confusion, poverty, strife, death, or loss of vision, vision interruption, or affliction. The Word of God pierces through the tactics of the enemy, whether that is your life or your whole family. It is your perception of the Word of God that makes the differences. The Word of God is "piercing even to the dividing asunder" This tells me that He knows how to separate us from the enemy and the things that come upon us or that we find ourselves amid.

I am reminded of my own story. You see, I was not supposed to be able to share, talk, or breathe. I watched God deliver me and my family. The word goes on to say that it "[divides] asunder of soul and spirit, joints [movement] and marrow [health], and it is a discerner of the thoughts and intents of the heart." This is so powerful when you can't move in your life, your mind, your spirit, your body. That is not living! God brings movement and health to us, to our whole self, and our whole lives. I started here because it is the foundation to any miracle, breakthrough, or blessing. Knowing the thoughts and intents of your own heart is important and key to any true and lasting 'Deliverance.'

Faith and Belief

—Hebrew 11:6, KJV but without faith it is impossible to please him. For he that cometh to God must believe that he is and that he is a rewarder of them that diligently seek him

It is in seeking this place of honesty and truth that you find Him. Seek Him regardless of the pain, regardless of who tells you not to because they do not believe in the Lord Jesus Christ of whom you keep speaking about.

2
Indictments

You know, the thing about indictments is this; Some were caused by the person, and some were inherited to no fault of the person. But I know and found in my own life that God is able in any case, to bring anyone into a [Mighty Deliverance] no matter where or what we are born into or for that matter find ourselves dealing with. But we will discuss this further in the chapters of this book.

He Is the Final Answer!

The whole chapter of Zechariah 3, was so blessed that the Holy Spirit impressed upon me to write of this man of God called Joshua because there were some things that were going on with Joshua, and he was the high priest, you see, no one is exempt from a battle with themselves. This Joshua was not Joshua the leader of Israel in the conquest of Canaan. This was the high priest after the Babylonian captivity. And the prophet Zechariah saw him in the spirit, standing before the presence of an angel of the Lord, and satan standing by to tempt him. So, the Lord rebuked satan, because his event was a representation of a restoration, and God refused to permit him to stop the restoration of Judah and Jerusalem.

Now, I have to stop there because God gave me such a revelation here: We see that this high priest had some garments on him that had to come off so that he can properly take the position that God had ordained for him to take. The point I am trying to make is that, there is a standard that he needed to represent before God and the people that were assigned to his ministry; and the behavior and movements that was not only in him but influencing the things around him was getting in the way of the plan and purpose God had for his life.

He was ministering with garments that were not acceptable nor proper for his calling. And thereafter, he was given a charge he would have to meet in order to be blessed; which was also indicative of the coming of the Messiah and salvation.

God can change anything that needs to be changed when you are submitted totally to God, with your whole heart, whole mind, and whole soul. This is the season to be transparent before God. This is the season to connect and not disconnect. Go beyond the veil.

It is time to rise! You cannot be weighed down with your "garments."

And God gave me this revelation: Some or most are walking around right now with filthy garments, and you can choose to take them off with the help of the Lord. My own story is one to be told. I had experienced the loss of a child through murder, kidnapping, rape, and many other abuses, but through the course of my life, those were indictments against me, and Satan was standing right there, not wanting me to receive my deliverance and I, at one point, did not want to receive it either. I was depressed and oppressed and suicidal and a lot of other things in those seasons. You see, Satan does not want us to experience the restoration and salvation to our individual lives, families, or the body of Christ for that matter. But he is a liar! For years some or all of you who are reading this book have be experiencing what I am talking about because God showed me, and He instructed me to let you know that: You can be delivered; the word of God states this in

Zechariah 3:4, KJV and he answered and spake unto those that stood before him, saying, Take away the filthy garments from him. And unto him he said, Behold, I have caused thine iniquity to pass from thee, and I will clothe thee with change of raiment] the verses go on to say in

Zechariah 3:5, kjv And I said, let them set a fair miter upon his head. So, they set a fair miter upon head, and clothed him with garments. And the angel of the LORD stood by.

So, as you read further down into the chapter God gave Joshua a charge to keep the ways and charge of the Lord and all the benefits described with take place. If you notice in this verse the specificity of the (head) it speaks to the mind there are so many people walking around in the world and in the Body of Christ that have minds that are not delivered or healed and shows me continually how there needs to be a mind deliverance. In further study of this event with Joshua it showed that this miter was not the normal one that the priest wore. This one was supernatural from God and it had a gold plate on the front of it that read "Holiness to the Lord". How many priests are pedophiles? How many pastors? And there are many more examples.

Wherever there is a garment that needs to be removed its time. Further indicating and revealing that there are instances in life that have happened and this induces the fact that even those garments must be changed as well in order for you to walk out your purpose and this book speaks to all aspects of having your garments changed and renewed by the Power of the Living God: It's even more of why GOD has impressed me write these words of Deliverance to you as a victim of people whose garments were spotted to the point of injury to others:

> *"I rose out a grave that the enemy had assigned for me to tell you that no weapon that has been formed against you shall prosper".*

[Isaiah 54:17, KJV]

[No weapon that is formed against thee shall prosper; and every tongue that shall rise against thee in judgment that thou shalt condemn. This is the heritage of the servants of the LORD, and their righteousness is of me, saith the LORD].

This is your season, your opportunity to change your life forever, and all that you must do is be honest! Whatever filthy garments you or anyone in your family is wearing God can deliver, and this is the powerful part. No matter if it is physical, mental, or psychological. Wherever you find yourself reading this book God can find you. Right there!

Come out of your chains!

If the Son therefore shall make you free, you shall be free indeed.
(John 8:36, KJV)

What I love about this scripture is the word *indeed*. The word *in* is expressing here a period when an event takes place, or the appearance of someone or something being enclosed or surrounded by something else. Instead of recognizing every negative thing that happens in your life, you need to understand that you have a *deed*. You understand when there is a legal document assigned to an individual concerning property, they receive a deed to that property that tells everyone that it belongs to them. Well, your healing, your deliverance, your breakthrough, your miracle belongs to you. This is the place where your life is going in circles day in and day out. When you are so confused and lost emotionally, and you are in total despair to the point where you can't see things clearly both within your inner eyes nor the eyes in front of you both are deceiving you. After you have gone through being raped or suffered the loss or murder of a loved one, or you felt so lonely you just did not want to live. "To the point where it felt as if no one could understand what you are going through: "Yes the place between going insane or actually crossing over into it and only God can bring you out. (A place that I am familiar with because God brought me out and to him, I am so thankful! I know he is a deliverer!!! "RIGHT THERE" are you in that position right now? Yes; that place called "THERE"

My Brother, my Sister I know him as the Balm in Gilead, my counselor, way-maker, savior, mind-regulator and heart fixer; battle fighter even when the pain and war within me was both unbearable and things were unexplainable to the finite mind and heart. Just as it is within you right now. Take a look at this scripture and let it comfort you as it did me:

[Matthew 6:22, KJV] The light of the body is the eye: if therefore thine eye be single, thy whole body shall be full of light.

"I ENCOURAGE YOU TO PRESS ON"

*God is our source. Do not go another moment, another second, minute, week, month, or year in that position. Turn it over and let **God bless you and your family's life.***

Prophets Pen:

I Preached a message called "The Work is Worth the results. The enemy will always use people to try and devalue the work that God has anointed you to do. The ministry God has given me pertaining to inner circle, regionally, nationally, and globally has been challenged on many levels. Whether by subliminal messages, being treated as if your ministry is not good enough while being compared to others to get a value of your worth is ludicrous.

Because you did not write a book of 100 pages and your wrote a book of 54 pages does not make you less than.

If you take on those thoughts you will dress yourself with defeat, doubt, and more.

The many books that God has anointed me to write as his prophetic scribe bring therapy, salvation, and deliverance and a wealth of Faith.

Never feel like you need to be someone else, Nor should you compare what God has put in you with another's purpose. Trust God to activate and manifest the purpose he has given you.

God told me without fail He said, Daughter keep doing what I have called you to do; to reach the multitudes. Reach the multitudes that I have assigned to this ministry.

[HEBREWS 10:35, KJV]

Cast not away therefore your confidence, which hath great recompence of reward.

3

Pressing On

I was studying the Word of God one day, and the Lord showed me something so powerful that I began to immediately meditate on this area with the Holy Spirit where it talked about the woman in the Bible with the issue of blood. But, you see, she was not the only one who was at the Lord's feet. Jairus was there as well, and he had a daughter who was dying, and right in the middle of his situation, right in the middle of the road of his life and his child's life, right in the middle of his perception, his prayer, his faith, his position, his promise and his praise, God showed up and changed their garments.

The Fruit of His Faith Manifested the Miracle: Luke 8:41–55

[41] And, behold, there came a man named Jairus, and he was a ruler of the synagogue and he fell down at Jesus' feet, and besought him that he would come into his house:[42] For he had <u>only one daughter</u>, about twelve years of age, and she lay a dying. But as he went the people thronged him. [43] And a woman having an issue of blood twelve years, which had spent all her living upon physicians, neither could be healed of any,[44] Came behind him, and touched the border of his garment: and immediately her issue of blood stanched.[45] And Jesus said, Who touched me? When all denied, Peter and they that were with him said, Master the multitude throng thee and press thee, and sayest thou, who touched me? [46] And Jesus said, somebody hath touched me: for I perceive <u>that virtue is gone out of me.</u> [47] And when the woman saw that she was not hid, she came

trembling, and falling before him, she declared unto him before all the people for what because she had touched him, and how she was healed immediately.

[48] And he said unto her, Daughter, "be of good comfort: thy faith hath made the whole; go in peace. [49] While he yet spake, there cometh one from the ruler of the synagogue's house, saying to him. Thy daughter is dead; trouble not the Master. [50] But when Jesus heard it, he answered him, saying, Fear not; <u>believe only</u> and she shall be made whole.[51] And when he came into the house, he suffered no man to go in, save Peter, and James, and John, and the father and the mother of the maiden. [52] And all wept, and bewailed her: but he said, Weep not; she is not dead, but sleepeth [53] And they laughed him to scorn, knowing that she was dead. [54] And he put them all out, and took her by the hand, and called, saying, <u>Maid, arise.</u> [55] And her spirit came again, and she arose straightway: and he commanded to give her meat.

And when you read this chapter, it is a miracle within a miracle because Jesus was on the way to Jairus's house in the first place. The woman with the issue of blood was considered an interruption. But oh, what a blessing for it to be an interruption and a blessing at the same time. The word of God tells us in James 1:4 (KJV), "But let patience have her perfect work that you may be perfect and entire, wanting nothing." Knowing what this word is in your language, you may say "I'm patient!" But it means being able to accept or tolerate delays, as well as suffering, without getting angry or upset. And we know that no one is perfect at that, but as you begin to understand things and walk in a truth about different aspects of life and circumstances, you will find yourself allowing patience to have her way. If you look at this word in the Hebrew language, it means "who is slow." When it comes to the process of deliverance or recovery, you must take time to walk out your own process, and as you see the ugly, the difficult, you press on anyway.

Forgiveness is a key component to this because most of the time we are born into situations or circumstances that we did not create, so forgive yourself for what you had no idea about but found yourself dealing with while trying to figure out; and navigate through your life at the same time. What we consider horrible at times is a blessing in disguise. Jesus shows us here that he was not so busy with Jairus situation that he could not take a moment to minister to the woman with the issue of blood (key word "*ISSUE*) He never said that his daughter was dying, but Jesus knew! And as he was on his way, Jairus met him in the middle of the road. ***Jesus will meet you in the middle of your situation,*** [no matter what road you are on] I pondered with the Holy Ghost about Jairus and his daughter and the Woman with the issue of blood and *12 years.*

I realized after the Holy Spirit led me to stop here and began to study out why these two miracles were so divinely connected and ordered strategically by God. The number 12 is one of the Numerics' in the word of God. That means that its appearance is significant, and the number appears several other places in his word. And on top of that there is a numerical structure to how our heavenly father orchestrates and does things; in both the old and the new testament. Believe it or not there are those who call God 'The Great Geometrician" a title that I agree with because time belongs to God. He measures things and he always has a plan either by weight, numbers or by measuring things out. Since God is the author of scripture, [2 Tim 3:16, KJV] All scripture is given by inspiration of God, and is profitable for doctrine, for reproof, for correction, for instruction in righteousness: so to me, He is the creator of the world as well, [Deuteronomy 10:14 Behold, the heavens and the heaven of heavens [is] the LORD'S thy God, the earth [also], with all that therein [is] meaning [all that is in it and on it]. He is the creator of the world as well, then the word of God and the works of God should harmonize. The intricate part of this number 12 is that the number 3 which is known as the divine number in connection with Holy things which is within this number and this event Representing the Father, Son, and the Holy Ghost and the trinity of man: Body, Soul and Spirit.

(Do you see the connection?)

But to go deeper it also represents Jesus (First Begotten From the Dead) So this led me to the number 4 which is representative of "The number of the World: but what I found here is that it also represented the seasons ones in which God is in control of: (Winter, Spring, Summer, Autumn) and it also represents the compass (north, west, east, south) God can find you in any season that you are experiencing at this moment in your life; we may not understand all of these things but God does and he shows up on time. [Acts 1:7, KJV] And he said unto them, It is not for you to know the times or the seasons, which the Father hath put in his own power.

Psalms 139:5 says: Thou hast beset me behind and before and laid thine hand upon me.

The word all-en-com-pass-ing when broken down means exactly what we seen here including or covering everything and everyone anytime. He wants to heal you just like Jairus's daughter and the woman with the issue of blood though it had been 12 years for the woman and the young girl was 12 years old they had an appointment with God just as you do reading this book and getting deliverance in the timing and harmony of the word and works of God. It is a critical peace as well when you see how Jesus was the first begotten from the dead. He is Resurrection and with him comes resurrection Jairus's daughter was dead and the woman with the issue of Blood was dying. "Look at God" wherever you have found yourself today it's time to "LIVE".

"LET'S GO A LITTLE DEEPER"

I know that there are times in our lives that as parents we do things that affect our children because of the lives lived before we had them or while we have them. And God is so merciful that I thought of Deuteronomy 24:15 (KJV): "The fathers shall not be put to death for the children, neither shall the children be put to death for the fathers: every man shall be put to death for his own sin." Whatever he needed to say to Jesus or to repent for he made it right! I know that you may not have thought of this, but that is my conversation with God. His faith for his daughter caused a reaction in Jesus, and she was healed. This was one of the rulers of the synagogue, a man of position who did not lack anything, but with all his prestige, he could not do anything to change his daughter's condition. There are things money can't buy.

Jairus reached out to this lowly Jesus who had all power in his hand. Jairus positioned himself humbly before the Lord! I could see him as he was at the feet and he did not move even through all the thronging that was going on. He held on to the Lord while the Lord was healing the woman with the issue of blood. I believe that it increased his faith even more. Sometimes things do not happen the way we want or when we want or how we want, but faith moves mountains, opens doors, and pulls down walls. Now, remember Jesus was on his way to his house, but he met Jesus. How are you positioning yourself to meet him? They lowered the man from the roof to Jesus. How bad do you want this change, this movement? The same way the anointing is meeting you in your house right now!

When you think you are not worth it or that he has no time or is too busy, think again. The Word goes on to tell us in Luke 8: 49, KJV

> [49] While he spake, there cometh one from the rulers of the synagogue's house saying to him, thy daughter is dead; trouble not the master. But when Jesus heard it, he answered him, saying, Fear not: believe only, and she shall be made whole.

Now, watch this! You must understand that Jesus heard someone say something to Jairus when you would have thought he did not hear him at all. This encouraged me so because people will try and get you off track and try and pull you out of your faith for the impossible. But God tells us to have singleness of the eye:

Mathew 6:22 (KJV): "The light of the body is the eye: if therefore thine eye be single; thy whole body shall be full of light."

This is such a powerful word to us from God because it tells us whatever is dark, get rid of it. The woman with the issue of blood had to not lean on the facts of her condition. Nor did Jairus stay in the symptoms of his daughter.

They gave their situations light by standing in their trust and faith in God.

John 11: 9-10 AMP Jesus answered, Are there not twelve hours in the day? Anyone who walks about in the daytime does not stumble, because he sees [by] the light of this world. [10] But if anyone walks in the night, he does stumble, because there is no light in him [the light is lacking to him] We must stand in the light of Jesus, Live in the Light, Breathe in the light, Move in the light of his word and awesome deliverance power. Your eyes sight must go from pain to power so that you will stop stumbling in the night seasons of your life as your night becomes daytime and you began to stand in the light of the Lord for it is then that the light is not lacking in us and we can move through the seasons of our lives courageously as Jairus and the woman with the issue of blood.

We either frame our world to fail or we frame our world in faith: "Through Faith we understand that the worlds were framed by the word of God, so that things which are seen were not made of things which do appear" (Heb. 11:3, KJV). You see, your inside thinking, and mind-set can be reframed from what the enemy has made you believe all these years whether from the age of five or fifty-five and beyond. Change is possible! You can go from trauma to triumph. Without faith, it is impossible to please Him. I believe God can heal you in every situation that you may have, every devastation, every circumstance, every unimaginable moment that you face. I have faced many of these moments, but God is so good that I stand in peace and happiness! So that you will understand that no matter the horror, the pain, the mind-blowing moments, he is the Balm in Gilead that heals us.

I could hear this man speaking to Jairus saying something like this: "Get up off your knees. It will not work. Your daughter is dead." Now, you must remember something: When he first met Jesus in the middle of the street, his daughter was *dying*. And now she is *dead!* His position blessed me again because we must not ever give up. I know that when Jesus had responded the way he did in these verses, he knew that Jairus was there the first time, and Jairus did not say, "Oh why is Jesus not stopping? I just want him to come to my house and forget that woman." As we go through things in life, patience is key and at the same time courage. You must have faith and trust because they go hand and hand. [Psalms 31:24, KJV] Be of good courage, and he shall strengthen your heart, all ye that hope in the LORD. Though it seems like God does not hear us, He does.

Delay Is Not Denial

He told Jairus, "Believe only." You must believe only to take off the garments of death that the enemy attempts to put on you or has put on your children, your family, that husband, that wife, or that ministry, etc. I had to believe only when I walked through those situations I spoke of earlier. I had to believe Him to deliver my mind, my heart, my body, and my soul. In Luke 8:51–55 (KJV), we see that Jairus had sent up some prayers, and God had made him some promises, regardless of the fact of persecution; praise was in effect.

"Your daughter is dead. That situation is dead and won't arise."
Not so!

You must believe regardless, just as Jesus did when he put them all out in knowing the young girl was sleep. Mathew 9:24 (KJV) reads, "He said unto them, give place: for the maid is not dead, but sleepeth. And they laughed him to scorn." Just like Jesus, when there are things around you that are not going to bring life to you, it is time for it to go. Even the four lepers in 2 Kings 7:3 (KJV) know. "There were four leprous men at the entrance of the gate: and they said one to another, why sit here until we die?" Some people, places, and things must change around you for this next level or stage of your life. Every stage of deliverance is important. And there are some instances when you are not strong enough; that's when you lean even further on "Daddy God" that's what I call Him; you may call Him Father, Helper, Sustainer, Way Maker, either way: God will show up for you. I am reminded of [Joshua 14] vs [8] Nevertheless my brethren that went up with me made the heart of the people melt: but I wholly followed the LORD my God. And because he positioned himself for the inheritance Moses pronounced this in vs [9] And Moses sware on that day, saying Surely the land whereon thy feet have trodden shall be thine inheritance, and thy children's forever, because thou hast wholly followed the LORD my God. vs [10] And now, behold, the LORD hath kept me alive, as he said, these forty and five years, even since the LORD spake this word unto Moses, while the children of Israel wandered: and now, lo I am this day fourscore and five years old. The Word of God goes on to show us Joshua in vs [11] As yet I am as strong this day as I was in the day that Moses sent me: as my strength was then, even so is my strength now, for war, both to go out, and to come in. Just like Joshua we must Wholly follow the LORD.

[wholly- in a whole or complete manner; completely; the exclusion of other things totally; fully].

Joshua was 40 years old when he went from [Kadeshbarnea]: wilderness of wandering] and as you read at 45 years old, he was still STRONG and confident in God's ability to sustain and keep him in any challenge he had to face.

So with that said, we too have to decide if we will take the way that God gives us so that we can come into what God has ordained for us before the foundation of the world; and not be wandering in the wilderness of our situations and circumstances.

Joshua did not follow the others He followed GOD wholly not half -way.

I remember in my own life where God removed every person that was an instrument against the purpose God has ordained for my life, and he is doing the same for you. And in this, He will realign things in your life, as he did mine, and at the end of the day, all you can say is "Thank you, Jesus!"

Getting rid of the unhealthy garments in our life is the key to our lasting deliverance. The most powerful thing about this is that it is not just outer clothing that God is speaking of. There are things that have blanketed our mind-sets and behavior to the point where day after day and month after month or year after year, the circle continues with no change until there is a truth and a light that says, "I do not want this. I want that!" Have humility in this hour to truly let God show you yourself in the raw so that you can truly become what God sees you as: "It is possible to be free in God.

The Word of God concerning Jairus goes on to say that He "took her by the hand" like the Lord took mine. In the same way, he wants to take yours, and he called to her saying, "Maid, arise." He has called us to arise by his spirit, and the word goes on to say that "her spirit came again," and He commanded them to give her meat (food, fuel). I pondered this for a moment because that was the first thing Jesus said once she was awaken, and He was specific. We must always nourish ourselves with the Word, prayer, praise, and, most of all, faith: this is what gets us through our trials and tribulations.

On my radio program [Look Up and Live! which airs every thursday@ 3:15pm on www.wokbradio.com while broadcasting, one day, the Lord gave me a message for the people and He told me to ask them: "What are you eating?" You must watch what you allow into your spirit, whether that be your eyes, your ears, or your mind, and heart. These are gates the devil uses as gateways or doors. If you eat confusion, negativity, doubt, fear, hate, gossip, you are going to get it. [Proverbs 18:21] Death and life are in the power of the tongue: and they that love it shall eat the fruit thereof. You can breathe again; you can rise out of any situation with the help of the Lord. It is time to rise from the bed that has held you all these years.

4
The Branch

When we understand *who we are* than we will begin to walk in *who we are*. This chapter of the book caused me to go into deep meditation because of the delicacy of the issues we will look at here for we are His People, His Chosen, A Royal Priesthood, His Children. [1 Peter 2:9, KJV]

But for you to understand the branch, we must first start with the origin of it all, the Messiah, the Lord Jesus Christ.

The word *messiah* originated with the prophet Isaiah. It reappears in the prophecies of Jeremiah when it refers to a future king in the line of David who's coming would bring judgment and righteousness. In Jeremiah 23:5–6 (KJV), which is after the captivity, the term *branch* was recognized as the title of messiah. And as you go over to Zechariah 3:8 (KJV), this had taken on prophetic, priestly, and kingly connotations. And this is what He must be to us all.

Why are you telling us this prophet? Well, the Holy Spirit of God wanted me to point out to you the fullness of Jesus Christ. Your first part of deliverance is understanding, knowing, and believing that He is! Not *was* or *might be*, but He *is* a rewarder of them who diligently seeks him. [Hebrews 11:6, KJV]

Diligence is the friend of faith. It requires diligence in God to begin to bring you into the revelation of His word and the manifestation of the victory that you are believing God for. It was something about this chapter that caused me to really search out what it was that the Holy Spirit of God wanted to reveal to me to reveal to you. We must know who we are, and you must know God for yourself.

[God is never realized immediately, He is always revealed].

To Whom Do You Belong?

You see, when I first came to the Lord, I wanted to know who this Jesus Christ was, who is this Messiah that I see people shouting for and about and speaking about, and how did He deliver them. I desired to know him for myself and for my life. If you bear with me a moment, I must build the foundation where the Lord is trying to take you. The scary part about this is that there are people who have been in God for a long time and still do not know who God is. When we learn through the study of the Word that Jesus is the True Vine for you to live through, you will get to the place called *there*, where we are to be a branch within a branch. When I began to study this out, it blessed me to see the revelation of His Word.

Genesis says that we are all made in the image of God. But what is that image concerning us? The Word of God also says to us that it is in Him that we live, move, and have our being. There are four aspects of our Lord and Savior character. Jeremiah , Isaiah, and Zechariah speaks about this: the Branch of David, the Branch of Jehovah, the Servant of the Branch, the Man of the Branch : As we move forward in this section you will see the different aspects of the branch as it pertains to us as believers.

This part of the book is so intricate, so I really need you to take note here: I have learned because of the way that God has guided me in my life that each step that we take in the word of God should be moving us into a position that always has us going higher in him; just like when we walk upstairs there should always be a new level, new dimension, new realms in God.

Who is this Branch? Well, the characteristics of Jesus are here in the Word of God. He is called the Branch of David in the Book of Mathew, the Messiah promised to the fathers, which go back to Abraham. And then, Joshua is referred to as the "Branch" in [Zechariah 3:8 KJV] in which the Lord declares he is bringing him forth; with his fruitfulness and life [John 15:5, KJV] He is the vine we are the branches.

You see the word branch in the Hebrew has several meanings such as a son, a builder of family, a name, a relationship, a descendant, people, a watcher. The Word of God in [Zechariah 3:9] speaks to us about the power of the Lord. The [stone] represents the Lord's strength to Joshua [which represents his strength to us], there is so much in this chapter; that God reveals as you began to study the scriptures you see that the [seven eyes] speaks to the fullness; perfection, wisdom and knowledge of Jesus Christ; and the words [engrave the graving] in this very verse crosses us over deeper into the power of his word : the word [*engrave*] is an imprint, impressed deeply, or to infix; to implant or insert firmly in something. The word [*graving*] is to carve or sculpt: God is so intricate in how he makes sure that as we read and study his word the [BIBLE] our basic instructions before leaving earth. We see that it is like doors that open continually to different realms of God in our lives to enhance and liberate us dimensionally and prophetically into the manifestations he has ordained for us. For it is here that we are made in his image [Genesis 1:27, kjv]

The word of God must be a living extension in our lives so that we can produce the spiritual fruit needed to walk out our purpose on this earth.

Let's go deeper!

[Phillipians 2:7-8, kjv] [7] but made Himself of no reputation, taking the form of a bondservant, and coming in the likeness of men. [8] And being found in appearance as a man, He humbled Himself and became obedient to the point of death, even the death of the cross. You see through my studies of God's word the cross is very significant to the garments that we either wear or take off. In this instance the cross should reduce the outer man to death breaking through the human shell that we have getting down to the inner [person]. Breaking our outer man which consists of our opinions, ways, cleverness, love of ourselves and the whole man. This breaking is very significant to the progress of removing the filthy garments thereby making the point of the cross a key point. This area of the Bible speaks of His acts more than His words. I know you are wondering where I am going with this. Just bear with me so we see the Branch, our Lord and Savior, in so many facets.

[Psalm 40: 7–8 KJV] states, "I come to do thy will, O God." The premise that is most spoken of is that of the "Son of Man," which plainly means that He was a true man. He was both the idea and our representation of this race. We call him the Savior of All Men and, at the same time, the Second Adam. Everyone is involved when it boils down to this fact, which makes him not just the Messiah of Israel but the "Son of God and Master" giving us the authority and power to conquer Satan for we are redeemed from his plans and traps by the blood of Jesus Christ.

I say all this to you because you cannot fight properly if you do not know who you have on your side or whose loins you come from. Your mother's womb was not the beginning of your delivery. God knew you before you were in her womb. Just think about that for a moment. John 1:1 (KJV) says that the Word "from the very beginning was with

God and himself was God." Then the Word of God goes on to tells us that "[He] became flesh and dwelt among us" (John 1:14, KJV). You must understand that because of all of this, nothing can hold you, and no garments, no matter how long you have been wearing them or they have been wearing you, "they cannot stay". [If you are ready for your clothes to change].

Messiah means "the anointed one" or "chosen one." The Great Messiah is anointed above his fellows, above any priest, prophet, or king who was anointed with oil and consecrated in their perspective office. Jesus Christ our Messiah embraces in Himself all three offices. He walked among them as both divine and human in the single person of Christ at the same time. This is known as a *hypostatic union*. In the Greek the word Fysi' means "nature."

Hebrews 1:3 (KJV) says to us, "Who being the brightness of his glory, and the express image of his person, and upholding all things by the word of his power, when he had by himself purged our sins, sat down on the right hand of the Majesty on High." Moreover, [Hebrew 1:4,KJV] Being made so much better than the angels, as he hath by inheritance obtained a more excellent name as they. Even God told [all] the angels to worship him. Glory to God! You see, I understand who my father is. Now it's your turn? Pertaining to your own Deliverance.

Christ as Prophet

A prophet of God is someone who reveals God, speaks for God, and communicates to people the truths that God wants them to know. This is not about religion. This is about relationship. How many times do you have to get on the prayer line and not see deliverance in your life or in your family? God is a deliverer to those who really want to be delivered. There is a humility in this. No pride, no lies, no false pretense, just honesty about what is really going on inside of you.

Jesus was sent to do the will of the Father (Luke 22:42; Mathew 11:27; John 8:28). Everything that a Man or Woman of God does must be measured by the example and integrity of the Lord Jesus Christ.

Christ as Priest

The priest were the ones in the Old Testament who offered sacrifices to God in order to cleanse the people of their sins and went to God on behalf of the people. The priest were the ones in the Old Testament who offered sacrifices to God in order to cleanse the people of their sins and went to God on behalf of the people. All these priests made atonements for the people: that was the old way. But Jesus Christ is the True Priest who offered Himself as a sacrifice [one time]. [Romans 5:11, KJV] And not only [so], but we also joy in God through our Lord Jesus Christ, by whom we have now received the atonement. [1 Corinthians 15:22, KJV] For as in Adam all die, even so in Christ shall all be made alive. He is also our high priest: [Hebrew 4:14, KJV] Since then we have a great high priest who has passed through the heavens, Jesus the Son of God, let us hold fast our profession. [15] For we have not a high priest which cannot be touched with the feeling of our infirmities: but was in all points tempted like as we are, yet without sin. This does not mean we do not fall short : [Romans 3: 23-24, KJV] for all have sinned and fall short of the glory of God; [24] Being justified freely by his grace through the redemption that is in Christ Jesus: so wherever you find yourself right now look who your priest is. He Forgives! And if you are reading this book and you do not know Jesus Christ for the pardon of your sins then I invite you to be saved: [Romans 10:9,KJV] That if you shalt confess with your mouth the Lord Jesus, and shalt believe in thine heart that God hath raised him from the dead, thou shalt be saved. Amen welcome to the kingdom of God!

Christ as King

A king is someone who has authority to rule and reign over a group of people.

1 Timothy 2:5–6 (KJV) reads, "For there is one God and one mediator between God and Men; the Man Christ Jesus. Who gave himself a ransom for all, to be testified in due time?" I had to go this way because before you tap into the Branch, you must understand the Branch which is also the Vine. You see, in the beginning we spoke of Jesus being the Branch which means that God sent such a line out to us in the roots of Jesus so that there is no excuse for not being delivered, no excuse for staying in a place that you want to leave [free yourself], no excuse to not believe. He is the water that you need forever. It's something about the water of Jesus that changes your whole life; anything outside of God becomes a dry place in our lives the bible says in John 4:14, KJV But whosoever drinketh of the water that I shall give [my word] shall never thirst: but the water that I shall give him shall be in him a well of water springing up into everlasting life.

You must drink this "WATER". This living water is what delivered my mind, soul and spirit from the trauma of the murder of my daughter and much more. It is this water that saved my mind from the traumas that tried to hold me hostage and in bondage of low self-esteem and mental abuse, as well as physical abuse that tried to plague my life. This water is healing water and can bring to you life instead of death. I further admonish you to look at [Proverbs 27: 19, KJV] As in water face *reflects* face, So a man's heart *reveals* the man.

You see, this is a pivotal point here because the word of God is saying that the water is clear and most of us know what it is like to look in water at a lake or pond where clearly we have seen our reflection. [face to face] . The same with our hearts which represents our feelings and thoughts become a reflection just as the water reveals the face to us; so does the heart to the man or woman : Who we are is ultimately revealed to others. Yet the true change [starts]with [us] It is with this [living water] we can be washed and cleansed and renewed.

*There is no one like the **Lord Jesus Christ**.*
*[The word **ONE** here means one in individuality]*
[Jeremiah 10:6, KJV]

He gave Himself for us, and the most powerful thing about this is that every time that we get through a situation and every time our Lord and Savior manifests that miracle and blessings in our lives or the lives of our family members, God testifies of His Son and who He is and who he could be in our lives. "For when God made promise to Abraham, since He had no one greater to swear by, He swore by Himself" (Heb. 6:13, KJV).

The Lord and Savior Jesus Christ constantly shows himself as prophet, priest, and king. You must know who He is. You must seek to know him for yourself; For in Him is life, health, and strength. [Acts 17:28, KJV] For in him we live, and move, and have our being; as certain also of your own poets have said, for we are also his offspring

5

The True Vine

John 15:1–4 (KJV) says, I am the true vine, and my Father [God] is the husbandman. Every branch in me that beareth not fruit he taketh away: and every branch that beareth fruit, he purgeth it, that it may bring forth more fruit. Now ye are clean through the word which I have spoken unto you. Abide in me, and I in you. As the branch cannot bear fruit of itself, except it abide in the vine: no more can ye except ye abide in me.

Jesus is the One who mediates, one who acts as a link between parties, an intercessor, peacemaker, harmonizer, one who brings things into harmonious agreement with another; He brings us from despair to hope, sickness to health, sadness to joy, poverty to wealth, He is the true vine for us to drink from and a well spring of life to those who want to be set free.

The only way to bear fruit—through and in Jesus Christ!
Is to Stay connected to the vine.

You see every branch in you that is not of God and that causes you to not be whole in mind, body, or spirit God will purge it, and then once you get delivered and start to bear fruit, he will purge it again to bring forth more fruit. The foundation and key to personal deliverance is you must abide in the true vine. Alcohol, drugs, man, nor woman, car, nor jewelry is the true vine. You must live in, dwell in, and believe in the one and only, our lord and savior Jesus Christ. This is where you produce good fruit, the good fruit of all that brings life to you and your family.

You must abide in truth in order to live. Jesus Christ is truth! The order of God must be implemented. Alignment must come back in your life. I know this for myself because traumas and circumstances tend to knock us out of alignment with purpose and with God. The Word of God tells us in Psalms 51:6, KJV Behold, thou desirest truth in the inward parts: and in the hidden part thou shalt make me to know wisdom. So, we find ourselves having to be unraveled from life's turns and toils; trauma and situations that plaques our minds, hearts, and souls literally must be removed, reborn and remade.

The point is that you must abide in the True Vine the way God intended for you to live. I know this for myself; you know your testimony. When I was labeled as a multiple trauma victim, there were times that I thought my life was over, and I believed that I had to tap into the vine of despair, no hope, loneliness, hurt, pain, anger, love-lessness whether from others or toward myself.

John 15:5 (KJV) says, "I am the vine ye are the branches; he that abideth in me and I in him the same bringeth forth much fruit: for without me ye can do nothing." [6] of the same chapter says, "If a man abides not in me, he is cast forth as a branch, and withered, and men gather them, and cast them into the fire, and they are burned."

These verses are so powerful to me because the Lord is speaking very audibly to us about Him being the true vine and the true source. The Lord imparts to us [His branches] the ointment and divine strength and virtue that we need in our lives. Not tarot cards, music icons, nor witchcraft, no soothsayer, no diviner or warlock is the true vine. And we are powerless to produce lasting fruit without Him, whether that fact is recognized or not. It is God who created us, and that will be known and respected one way or another for it is [He] who have made us and not we ourselves (Psalm 100:3, KJV).] We must understand who we belong to, and until that happens, there will be chaos as well as confusion. You see, John 15:7 KJV goes on to say, "If ye abide in me, and my words abide in you, ye shall ask what ye will and it shall be done unto you" (KJV). [Verse 8] continues, "Herein is my father glorified, that ye bear much fruit; so, shall ye be my disciples" (KJV). We are made disciples through trials and tribulations while on our way to purpose and Destiny.

These experiences were a great lesson for many of our brother and sisters in the bible. And the great lesson for us to understand is that we must not only yield to God, but we must strive to complete the assignment God has given to us.

The sad part is that there are many branches that never make it because they abide in the wrong vine. Some get devoured by people or find themselves cast into many different dilemmas or situations unable to get out for fear or for other reasons they are trapped. Therefore, you must realize at some point that if you touch fire, you will get burned. It costs too much not to stay connected to the True Vine, our lord and savior Jesus Christ.

Why hinder your own progress by your own actions? or the actions of others? For in Him is life everlasting, He is alpha and omega, the beginning and the end of all things.. If the believer is fruitful, he is purged to produce more fruit. If the believer is fruitless, he is taken away or removed from being part of the vine.

That is the bottom line.

6
Wild Grapes

Isaiah [the prophet's] writings are a very precise; and to the point chapters which consists of [66] which corresponds with the [66] books of the bible this fascinates me: Isaiah's vision makes God's message really clear to the people of Israel . Isaiah s speaks of these things and God deals with them about their behavior as covenant people who in this case are persisting in sin but also brings them into the fact that the final process concerning them and God can be one that brings them to their restoration in the Messiah [Jesus Christ].

[Isaiah 5: 1-7] Now will I sing to my well-beloved a song of my beloved touching his vineyard [us]. My well-beloved hath a vineyard in a very fruitful hill:

[2] And he fenced it, and gathered out the stones thereof, and planted it with the choicest vine, and built a tower in the midst of it, and also made a winepress therein: and he looked that it should bring forth grapes, and it brought forth wild grapes.

[3] And now, O habitants of Jerusalem and men of Judah, judge, I pray you, betwixt me and my vineyard. [4] What could have been done more to my vineyard, that I have not done in it? Wherefore, when I looked that it should bring forth grapes, brought it forth wild grapes? I can see that it was the next couple of verses that Isaiah was in his chosen Prophetic assignment and God was using him to speak even deeper to the people because God was inquiring in the 4th verse bringing the people to the question concerning themselves but at the same time dealing with them. [5] And now go to; I will tell you what I will do to my vineyard: I will take away the hedge thereof, and it shall be eaten up; and break down the wall thereof, and it shall be trodden down: [6] And I will lay it waste: it shall not be pruned, nor digged; but there shall come up briers and thorns: I will also command the clouds that they rain no rain upon it. [7] For the vineyard of the

Filthy Garments

LORD of hosts is the house of Israel, and the men of Judah his pleasant plant: and he looked for judgment, but behold oppression; for righteousness, but behold a cry.

Isaiah sang a song to the Lord because he loved him so much he did not want to be identified with what was getting ready to happen to these people and he needed God to know that he still belonged to God and he wanted nothing to do with what was about to go down. This made me to shutter on the inside because God is so sovereign; I dare not challenge or disobey because I understand who God is. The people of Jerusalem and the men of Judah and the leaders of the tribes disregarded God. The house of Israel and the men of Judah had so much injustice, oppression and bloodshed; and distress that there was a great cry for mercy coming up to God. So He sent his Prophet [Isaiah] to pronounce the judgment that was about to happen in the following verses you see all that would happen [take a minute and read the rest : [8-14] spells out the judgment desolate houses, the poor being vindicated, crops not yielding prosperously, the fields that yielded ten bushels will produce one bushel my God!, the people will be turned over to the enemy without knowing it because they have no knowledge [of God]. The honorable men are famished and their common people are thirsty; they were released to [Sheol] which is [HELL] the unseen state and realm of the dead has an appetite that is unleashed and enlarged and its mouth is opened against Jerusalem . Everything that is tumultuous everyone that was great brought low, common men bowed down and the haughty minded were humbled. Now this was once a fruitful place that had it all and was blessed of God, but they didn't want to change those garments [attitudes are garments and it cost them everything]. [15-30] here God begins to share just who He is and tells the people through the Prophet of God that the Lord of Host is exalted in Justice , and God, the Holy one, shows himself holy in righteousness and through righteous judgments. And the following verses spell out in detail who specifically is doing what and what the punishment is?

- Woe to those who bring calamity, cords of iniquity, and falsehood
- Those who tempt God by wanting him to hurry up and prophesy and get it over with; to see vengeance that they may see it and know it.
- Woe to those who call evil good and good evil
- Who put darkness for light and light darkness?
- Those that put bittersweet and sweet bitter
- Those who justify the wicked for reward and take away the righteousness of the righteous from him; therefore as fire devoureth the stubble and flame consumes the chaff their root will be rotten; their blossom goes up in dust because they have

cast away the law of the LORD of hosts, and despised the word of the Holy One of Israel.

The anger of the LORD as you can see was kindled against the people and he had stretched forth his hand against the people, smitten them. As I read of these verses at length; I shook my head and saw how they had no fear of our creator they literally tempted God and minimized his power in their minds. [Isaiah :26-30] Then God raised up an army with their own ensign [a signal or point /flag placed on a high- mountains for the [rendezvous]- which is: a meeting at agreed time and place. For the [irruption] which means: to rush in forcibly or violently] they were literally wiped out: due to disobedience. As you go in and read the verses you can see just how and what they brought upon themselves.

[Hebrew 10:31, KJV] It is a fearful thing to fall into the hands of the living God.

Remember: Jehovah-God had a vineyard in a very fruitful hill, he fenced it, gathered out the stones from it, planted it with the choicest vine, built a tower in the midst of it, made a winepress in it, again he expected it to bring forth good grapes and it bought forth wild grapes.

So, God asked Judah these things:

1. Judge between them and His vineyard and decide certain matters.
2. Tell Him what he should have done that he had not done to make a vineyard produce good grapes.
3. Tell Him why they brought forth wild grapes when He had planted the choicest vine.

Making it Plain:

[Who is to blame for wild grapes? Is it God's fault? [OR!] Is it your fault?]

Oh, that we would just do the will of God: for God tells us in his word:

[2 Chronicles 7:14,KJV] If my people, which are called by my name, shall humble themselves, and pray, and seek my face, and turn from their wicked ways; then will I hear from heaven, and will forgive their sin, and will heal their land.

God will bring you to yourself one way or the other when you can go inside of yourself to find the answers. In honesty, humility and truth, you can bring forth good grapes, not wild grapes. God gave them the opportunity to look at all He had done. All that He had given them protected them from harm and put them in safety. The word *wild* here in the above scripture in Jeremiah means:

- Living independently of God
- Not domesticated or tamed: growing in a natural state not cultivated
- Uninhabited or uncultivated
- Desolate

"Nothing from nothing leaves Nothing"
It is time for change, you know it! God knows it! Now do something about it.

You see, I realized, when God saved me through His love and kindness and mercy that only He can give, that there was no ignoring what He has done and there was no turning back. For God I live and for God I will die. I am sold out to the Lord. Nothing should be able to separate us from Him when you are in the truth of who He is. There comes a point in life where you must intelligently decide about your relationship with God. Your relationship should always be moving in the forward direction of covenant. And our lives should not just be giving to Him some parts of our lives, but He must have all accessibility to us. Because if He does not, then we begin to run our own destiny and that is confusion.

[1 Corinthians 14:33, KJV] For God is not the author of confusion, but of peace, as in all churches of the saints.

Look at what is happening now in your life. You can't hide. He knows all things, and you cannot go another year in a lie. As you read on in chapter 5 of Isaiah, this sea of people had drunkenness, iniquities, pride, injustice, apostasy, and drinking. They were dressed in many things. What are you dressed with? Wild grapes?

God decreed these judgments upon Judah, and it is still true today:

- He will take away the hedge from it.
- The vineyard shall be beaten up.
- He would break down the wall from round about it.
- The vineyard shall be trodden down.
- He will lay it waste.
- There will be briars and thorns.
- He will command to the clouds that there will be no rain.

God *judgeth* the righteous, and God is *angry with the wicked every day:*

This means everyone. I can see individuals that continue in their stubbornness towards God for years. God warns the righteous and the wicked alike, and He is constantly directing us to go in the right direction. Just because you are a grown man or a grown woman, it does not mean you are above God or His correction. He created us, whether you are young or old. You cannot get around God. It is in *yielding* that you find true *freedom.*

When you can get past your own mind-set, your own stiff neck, and stiff-hearted self, you will began to experience this word: " O taste and see that the LORD is good: blessed is the man that trusteth in him. [Ps. 34:8, KJV]. When you take refuge in God and you get to the point in your life where you can get past your own flesh, you will not need to go down certain roads and neither will you desire to because you did not need to go down them in the first place. But that child inside rages like a child sitting on a chair having a tantrum, thinking they know better than God. Many lessons can be avoided. Not all but some we cause to happen to ourselves even after the warning.

Why is it so hard to listen? It is something that never leaves us since our childhood. I shake my head because I have experienced the season of being disobedient until God made it real clear to me; just as He is doing with you right now, until I made the conscious decision to obey for the exchange for obedience are blessings. [Luke 11:28 ,KJV] He replied, "Blessed rather are those who hear the word of God and obey it."

[Colossians 3:10,KJV] And to put on the new man, which is renewed in knowledge after the image of him that created him: We renew our knowledge and renew our minds with the help of God's word: [Psalms 1:2, KJV] But his delight is in the law of the LORD: and in his law doth he meditate day and night.

Thereby beginning and implementing the process of removing those filthy garments that must be removed at this season in the lives of those God is speaking to at this time. Colossians really brings to light just how much this scripture [3:10] is a wrap around for the others scripture it accompanies to simply say: "THEY NEEDED TO GET IT TOGETHER!'

What is so startling about this behavior is that our unified enemy puts people in his *[imagination]*. The word of God says in: [2 Corinthians 5: 10:5, KJV] Casting down the imaginations, *[notice the comma behind the word: representing a place]*; and every high thing that exalted itself against the knowledge of God, and bringing into captivity every thought to the obedience of Christ; the word of God goes on to show us in: [Ephesians 6:12, KJV] For we do not wrestle against flesh and blood, but against principalities, against powers, against the rulers of darkness of this age, against spiritual hosts of wickedness in the heavenly places. These agents of satan will always show you things that are contrary to the will of God. So the enemy presents images *[snap shots]* in your mind to get you to act upon those images and feelings, which lead to pictures that he places before you, like for some reason, you are not going to make it through that court situation. Your child or children will be devoured, that sickness will never leave your body, and lastly, the purpose God has given you will never see the light of day, and even as far as God does not love me, nor will He support me. "I might as well stay like this because I will never change."

That is a lie!

[2 Corinthians 11:14,kjv]
And no marvel; for Satan himself is transformed into an angel of light.

You must cast down these thoughts and visions that the enemy plaques you with. We must fight with the spiritual weapons God has given us because they are affective, and they are real and powerful. You must have confidence and faith in what God has given us. [Hebrews 10: 35, KJV] Cast not away therefore your confidence, which hath great recompence of reward. He teaches our hands to war and our fingers to fight. [Psalms 144: 1, KJV] Blessed be the LORD my strength, which teacheth my hands to war, and my fingers to fight: God will guide and lift you in his word, in praise , and in worship these are our weapons in God. You may be saying, "What does this have to do with me getting rid of my filthy garments?" There is a truth that you must be able to walk in and live in when it comes to our inner selves because those inner garments become outer garments. Those garments come in many forms they may be ancestral, a certain way of thinking or acting that must change in your life, or a traumatic circumstance that has haunted you for years and you cannot get away from it. You find yourself having flashbacks, snap shots that shape your mind into negative ways of thinking and living your life never coming out of the nightmare you are stuck in.

Do not believe the lies of Satan! My brother, my sister, man of God, woman of God, Apostle, Prophet, Pastor, Evangelist, Minister, Preacher, Teacher, God is no respecter of persons' circumstances, and trials find us all. No one is exempt from growing. We should all be learning and reaching for our best self in God. You must cast down those thoughts and everything that comes with it.

Fear has torment. [Proverbs 1:33, KJV] But whoso hearkeneth unto me shall dwell safely; and shall be quiet from fear of evil. The quality of life God wants us to enjoy is ruined, spoiled, and interrupted by [fear]. God will never leave His children, neither will he forsake us.

Proverbs 18: 21 (KJV) reads, "Death and Life are in the power of the tongue, and those who love it will eat its fruit."

We must do just as the word directs us to do—walk toward a road and mind-set of God. What conversation are you having with yourself concerning your situations? Where is your life right now?

The Scripture clearly tells us to not let our conversation be full of covetousness. *What are you saying, Prophet?* When you covet something, you yearn to possess or have something; to covet is to desire wrongfully. Now, follow me for this is how the Lord spoke this. When an individual begins to speak about what God cannot do in their life when God is either in the midst of working the situation out, or when they speak in a way not to even give God the opportunity to work it out and they speak negative and move negatively, then they are speaking defeat and death over their own lives and possibly their family, ministry and destiny as a whole those movements and those behaviors they become dressed in.

[It has become their clothes] at times [without due regard; for themselves or the rights of others]

So, if you habitually have negative talking— some other examples:
I need this to happen now," "This is not going to happen for me it is always like this,"—you are dressed to the point where you wear depression and oppression. "It's not happening fast enough, so I am going to do it myself." It is possible to covet our own behavior and wear those clothes to the point where you have become what you say.

God in this book is reaching out so that it will be understood that mind-sets and ways of thinking and navigation of the mind seem to be the origin for these behaviors. There are mind-sets that become possessions to the point where the person does not want to let go, like a Rolls-Royce or Mercedes, something so valuable that after you have it a long time, you cannot so easily let it go, but there comes a point when you cannot afford to keep it. As a matter of fact, it has always been a struggle to keep it financially; it straps you and maintenance is a killer. But you have become accustomed to the vehicle, and no matter how much it hurts you or causes you not to pay your other bills, you still want it, no matter the headache it has caused you and maybe to other to. "I am not doing it. There must be another way. I do not want to change for no one." It is the same with our words and behavior or a person's way of life. What are you saying to yourself and to others and where are those words and mind-set taking you? [Proverbs 14:12, KJV]

Take a minute and examine yourself at this point because God's words guide us into all truth. There is a transparent place that we must be in God where excuses end, and growth begins because it causes us to be content with such things we have. For our abundance is not in our own things; it is in God (Luke 12:15, KJV).

You see, people of God, I have lost much in my lifetime—possessions, family members, and all sorts of things. People have walked out of my life that I trusted. I have been in front of thousands and felt like I was alone. And God's abundant grace, love, and peace found me in a state that seemingly was not repairable. So, my conversation is with God and in God and for God. Philippians 2:5 (KJV) reads, "Let this mind be in you which was also in Christ Jesus." Let the action of emptying yourself begin so that you can take on the mind of Jesus Christ. Though this does not happen overnight, you must lay the brick to the foundation so that there can be a change in your life because it starts with you.

7
Well-Beloved

In the earlier chapters of the book, we talked about Isaiah speaking to a body of people a people that disobeyed God to the point where multitudes were destroyed. But the word beloved struck me because the same way that Isaiah was toward God is the way that we should all behold Him. Isaiah 5:1 (KJV) tells us, "Now will I sing to my *well-beloved* a song of my *beloved* [emphasis added]." The reason why this touched me so is because we are God's vineyard. My heart, my mind, and my soul sing a love song to the Lord. Isaiah was singing a love song to God, and the word well-beloved means that he or she:

Accepts God: generally approved God
Acclaimed God: praise enthusiastically and publicly
Admitted God: confessed to be true
Adored God: worship, love, and respect deeply
Advocated God: publicly recommend or support
Applauded God: praise by clapping, showing strong approval

Isaiah's heart in this verse caused my own expression of love for God to kick in because I love God so much for giving us his son as a ransom so that we would have the opportunity for abundant of life. [Mark10:45, KJV] For even the Son of Man came not to be ministered unto, but to minister, and to give his life as a ransom for many. It is good for us to accept God's love and devotion because it shows that we approve God and that we acclaim and praise enthusiastically who He is and what He had done in our lives. We admitted to God and confessed the miracles and blessings over the years that He has done despite sins committed. We adore and worship as well as respect Him so deeply that it comes out of our being as a shining light, thereby advocating and applauding Him. At times I am so overwhelmed by God and His presence. I bless him and thank him because he is well-beloved, and I constantly sing a song to my beloved. You must have gone through something to understand how the hand of the Lord can reach down and save you from the deepest part of the earth. [Deuteronomy 32:10, KJV] He founded him in a desert land, and in the waste howling wilderness; he led him about, he instructed him, he kept him as the apple of his eye. He loves me so much just as He loves you. Humbly, I write this book to encourage you and to push you forth in the spirit from the inside out for you to know God the Father and God the Son and God the Holy Spirit. To know yourself, you must know Him from the inside out.

> [Job 38:36, KJV] Who hath put wisdom in the inward parts?
> or who hath given understanding to the heart?

> *"Think on this for a minute"*
> *The answer: 'God does!' when we open ourselves to his will not our own!" He is wisdom and he know our hearts and he does give understanding. Still yourself to hear what God is relaying to you.*

> *[Proverbs 3:18, KJV] She is a tree of life to them that lay hold upon her: and happy is every-one that retaineth her.*

> *Also:*

> *[Proverbs 4: 5, KJV] Get wisdom, get understanding: forget it not; neither decline from the words of thy mouth.*

Trust and Believe

[Proverbs 13:13-14 KJV] Whosoever despiseth the word shall be destroyed: but he that feareth the commandment shall be rewarded.

[14] "The law *[teaching]* of the wise is a fountain of life *[natural source of living water]*, to depart from the snares of death.

[Psalms 36:9, KJV] For with thee is the fountain of life: in thy light shall we see light.

God *[our creator]* is all-knowing *[omniscient]*: He has been here before our existence; it is this fountain *[source of life and vigor]* that blesses us to continue to live, to live prosperously, to be quickened and restored and preserved in life: which is to us God very breathe to help with any situation or circumstance no matter the height or depth of them.

[Romans 8: 38-39, KJV] For I am persuaded, that neither death, nor life, nor angels, nor principalities, nor powers, nor things present, nor things to come, [39] Nor height, nor depth, nor any other creature, shall be able to separate us from the love of God, which is in Christ Jesus our Lord. The guidance and wisdom of God keeps us from the snares that have been set before us. I am living proof, as well as others, that He will deliver you from [all] snares. You must trust and believe.

8
New Again

I did not understand it, but I realized that being in line with the thoughts that God had for me was greater than I could even think. You see, from the moment that my father left, and my sister died, and my daughter was murdered, my life was full of running, protecting myself and my children, and making sure that I stayed in God no matter what. It was a season of growth as well as great warfare seemingly all the time.

In times of loss, fear, abandonment and times of making sure that my household was safe and in the covering of God, I, through all of this, learned to trust God with all my life.

2 Corinthians 5:17 (KJV) reads, "[Behold] old things have passed away; behold, all things are become new." When you behold something, you clearly open your heart to perceive what God is doing in your life and it is what God says that it is. You can be in an old thing so long that you may have scales on your eyes and cobwebs on your heart. [Acts 9:18, KJV] And immediately there fell from his eyes as it had been scales; and he received sight forth-with, and arose, and was baptized. And at that point you will either step into what God has for you or you will abort or forfeit it. God's love is so awesome that his love is the seed that causes all things to grow. When it seems as if your life is over, He makes things new again.

There were people along the way that God sent as agents and mentors that shifted my life and ministry both dimensionally and prophetically. I thank God for them, some I may never see again, but God put them on assignment for my life. You may be in the midst of your transition right now; it is good to know where you are when you are in the midst of transition—transition of your eyes, heart, mind, soul, and, yes, your garments[some clothes are harder to take off than others but do the work it's worth it. I preached a message a short time ago called **"The Work is Worth the Result!"**. And that transition could look so *devastating* that it seems like your *destruction and death,* but it is your destiny *to be delivered.*

I know that there was a lot said, but I must follow the leading of the Holy Spirit because many people of different backgrounds / personalities are being ministered to.

There are many garments that people wear. Whether saved or unsaved, there is no difference because deliverance is deliverance whichever way you slice it. I rose from the ashes by the grace of God to tell you that the Lord is able, to help you change your garments of pain, suffering, trauma, loss that has caused you to not be able to move in your life. Causing stagnation in your life because of abuse, low self-esteem, hatred, and bitterness -all these attributes can cause the flow of God to be hindered because of the inner war as well as your health and everything around you being placed in jeopardy. Mentally you are not free to even be who God has called you to be. Though I had so many traumas in my life the power of God unwrapped my mind from the filthy garments that the enemy had assigned for my life to stifle and hinder me. God is more powerful.

You do not have to continue day in and day out with the same mindset, behavior, or lifestyle choices. Are you ready to change today?

God Delivers

God is able. He took me from a place of poverty in spirit to wealth everlasting, from a place of despair, from the murder of my child to a place of love and hope, from a place of being kidnapped and raped to a cleanliness that only God can give. These are just some of the garments that God changed in my life. You know the garments the enemy has placed on your mind and heart and soul that you want God to deliver so that you can live.

As I said earlier, if He can do it for me, He can do it for you. Just let Him in now. Whether you have to receive the Lord Jesus Christ as savior of your life and surrender, whether you have made gods of your pain to the point that you will not let God be lord over your life even though you know that He is the creator, there is a repentance that must take place.

1 John 1:8-10 (KJV) tells us,
"If we say that we have no sin, we deceive ourselves and the truth is not in us. If we confess our sins, he is faithful and just to forgive us our sins and cleanse us from all unrighteousness. If we say that we have not sinned, we make him a liar, and his word is not in us."

Romans 14:8 (KJV) says further to us,
"For whether we live; we live unto the Lord; and whether we die, we die unto the Lord; and whether we live therefore, or die we are the Lord's." We are the created by the Creator whether you believe this or not. God has revealed and opened the inner man or woman in you, and I pray that you will repent and that you would give God yourself and your family. I pray that you would give Him your innermost mind, heart, and soul

Prayer of Release

Lord, change the garments that need to be changed and remove the garments as they release them unto you from their mind, spirit, heart and soul. Let the oil of your anointing move as healing salve through their whole-being. Bring healing now! Bring deliverance now! Uproot now! Save now!

Touch every child being prayed for, every wife, husband, and family member. Move, Lord, like You moved in my life. Open doors of recovery to everyone. Open the portals of heaven and let your angels go before them as they pray sincerely for the work is worth the result. Help them to do the inner work that will change their outer situations. Help them to be honest about what is going on inside of them and make the changes necessary with your help to really come to the fullness and knowledge of you.

I ask, God, that You would open the eyes of them standing there, that they stop blaming others for what is going on in them and stop judging others for their past, and that they move from their past with your help and cause a yielding that brings forth the miracles within the mind, soul and spirit I thank you now for your anointing that brings deliverance : you know what they need and the way they are feeling and I pray for complete and total wholeness in Jesus Name. Amen.

Know that you are all in my thoughts and prayers continually. May God richly bless you is my prayer for He who the son has set free is free indeed. [John 8:36, AMP] So if the Son liberates you [make you free men], then you are really and unquestionably free. It is clear that freedom is not in the word alone ; its our relationship to Jesus Christ and abiding in His Word. [Stay Free]

Your Friend and Servant of God,

Prophetess Sonya James